MIASMAMIST

QUERENCIA

MIASMAMIST

tommy wyatt blake

Querencia Press – Chicago IL

QUERENCIA PRESS

© Copyright 2025
tommy wyatt blake

ISBN 978 1 963943 37 5

www.querenciapress.com

First Published in 2025

Querencia Press, LLC
Chicago IL

Printed & Bound in the United States of America

contents

thanks for the business card?   9
howl (1)   10
hypnagogia   11
don't breathe   12
howl (2)   13
red aura in the periphery   14
mona lisa is jealous   15
angel or ghoul? quiz   16
wallflowers in the attic   17
another space poem   18
sans femme, hollywood   19
you asked me to write you a poem   20
s-s-surreal, oscillating / how to have sex with a transguy   21
wait, can i see that business card again?   22
need an ouija board to talk to you   23
post-titanic confessional   24
"don't forget to lubricate the corpse!"   25
lucky for you   26
you better be joking   27
creation myth   28
bloodbath   29
the door   30

thanks   32
about the author   33

thanks for the business card?

"trust me, i'm a mortician:

when you grow tired
of dragging around
your own corpse,
call me."

howl (1)

the wolf wears
my vertigo well:
sheepsoft clouds
trip over poppies
a little treat
for naked dreams

while crows eat
red moon
and twig-
snapping howls
smoke the whole forest
like a well-packed bowl.

hypnagogia

my cocked jaw
protrudes

into the consciousness
of others,

a half-lucid
luck of the draw

slinks me back
to a daydreamer's void.

don't breathe

your upright jaw
thrusts on
a longbow
that struck my mind
unstrung; –

you tell me
i don't need to breathe
when i'm already
hung from the moon,
stunned by insomnia.

howl (2)

the wolf goes down
to the lake, begs
it to drown
their conscience.

it delivers—
morning wood
rotting from moldwater
splinters their mouth,
coldcocked
and raw.

red aura in the periphery

crystal ball eyes project
a vision in microcosms
of dust: vessels of body—
the topography of mine—
breaking to red
in the palms of your hands.

mona lisa is jealous

fill me
like a canvas,
my blood
like paint
spilling
from your stiff
brush.

angel or ghoul? quiz

pick a vibe:

feeling	/	*emptying*
like	/	*to*
an	/	*a*
angel	/	*ghoul*
who	/	*when*
needs	/	*there's*
to	/	*the desire*
save	/	*to*
someone	/	*lose*

wallflowers in the attic

*i've caved into
vintageburned floral
wallpaper—
to be invisible.*

*breathing wanes
as flowers fade
yellowed, the insulation
pilling with white—*

*unrequited,
and this is the way
it should be.*

another space poem

*did you know i would give you
the universe if you wanted,
make every dimension
in your image? i am so sorry
your world is too small
for us
to exist in it.*

sans femme, hollywood

fuck me in french
and don't you dare
paint me like a lady.

you asked me to write you a poem

i've split into versions
of myself and all of them
still want to fuck you.

s-s-surreal, oscillating / how to have sex with a transguy

*torrid waves die
on the coastline
just to tremble
a little, just to
breathe it all
just one time.*

wait, can i see that business card again?

rotting is an inside job
and you don't care
for a career change.

need an ouija board to talk to you

why can't i horny away
the horrors   why do i fear
and love   the same
can't i tap into   some   third space
a chasm   of uncertainty   is fine
so long as   needles of wind   froth at the top
your voice howling   faintly   in patches
of sun   circling it   after three beats
and i'd give   anything   if it means yes
and i'd give   anything   for you
*   to trace   over my lips   again*

post-titanic confessional

i know what it looks like,
the ocean bluing
around my neck
into a locket, my nude
hairy nipples
in crisp detail—and you
tell me you want to draw me
like one of the girls???

"don't forget to lubricate the corpse!"

if you fuck me bonedry
one more time, you
will never cum again.

lucky for you

like a zombie,
if i soak my bones
and shake them
in the sun, i won't
be stonecold
anymore.

you better be joking

*do you really
want to writhe
in a graveyard
of verdigris vaginas,
buried in a coffin
of cum?*

creation myth

*i am waiting
for the void
beyond the sky
spinning
a tepid bath
of gray dust
and starlight,
a vulnerable
way to say:*
this isn't for you.

bloodbath

acrid wavelengths
of your skin
miasmamists
with the smell
of your genitals.
when was the last time
you took a bath;
was it when you
split the womb open,
all no holes
or one great void,
all bloodied
with ghostpiss?

the door

i cut off my girlbody
just to watch your cat
drag it back in.

i won't walk back
into a carcass again.

leave the dead
at the door
alone, don't tend

to its form with your fingers
bare and taunt me
to say how it feels.

thanks

i am incredibly grateful for nat, arden, dre, and vee. thank you for your love, support, and care.

special shout to elena, who inspired me to return to this manuscript almost 10 years after it was originally written. thank you for teaching me how to stop abandoning the past.

special shout to emily perkovich, the editor in chief of Querencia Press, who regifted this book a home.

& many thanks to my cats—princess, cosmo, and toast.

about the author

tommy wyatt blake (he/they) is the jester of popular culture and poet laureate of timefuckery. he's the author of DITCHLAPSE / [REALLY AFRAID]; NOW THAT'S WHAT I CALL HORROR!; So, Who's Courage?; Trick Mirror or Your Computer Screen; disasterfire/disasterstar; and others. they are currently synthesizing digital archives, space voids, and confines of the body.

other books written by tommy wyatt blake:

- *DITCHLAPSE / [REALLY AFRAID]* **(Querencia Press)**
- *system mapping* **(A Moonlit Cafe)**
- *NOW THAT'S WHAT I CALL HORROR!* **(Gutslut Press)**
- *TASEREDGED (watch out!)* **(Querencia Press)**
- *TAKE THIS QUIZ! 11 questions to see if you agree with courage as a metaphor* **(Ghost City Press)**
- *So, Who's Courage?* **(bullshit lit)**
- *space cowboy on a little, uh, space exploration?* **(Bottlecap Press)**
- *lacuna* **(kith books)**
- *Trick Mirror or Your Computer Screen* **(fifth wheel press)**
- ***...& more***

www.ingramcontent.com/pod-product-compliance
Lightning Source LLC
Chambersburg PA
CBHW060957120626
46557CB00003B/1196